AN ANSWER TO
FAMILY COMMUNICATION

by

Norman Wright

Harvest House Publishers
Irvine, California 92714

Unless otherwise noted:
Scripture quotations are from The Amplified Bible: Old Testament, ©by Zondervan Corp.; The Amplified Bible: New Testament, ©by Lockman Foundation, 1954, 1958 and are used by permission.

Scripture quotations are from the New American Standard Bible, © The Lockman Foundation 1960, 1962, 1963, 1968, 1971, 1972, 1973, 1975 and are used by permission.

Scripture quotations marked TLB are taken from The Living Bible, ©Tyndale House Publishers, 1971, Wheaton, Illinois. Used by permission.

AN ANSWER TO
FAMILY COMMUNICATION

©1977 by Harvest House Publishers,
Irvine, CA 92714
Library of Congress Catalog Card
Number 76-52832
ISBN 0-89081-031-1

Printed in the United States of America

AN ANSWER TO
FAMILY COMMUNICATION

Communicate? How, when you get nothing but the great stone wall? Your spouse won't talk, won't listen—nothing but grunts or "uh-huhs." Or perhaps your spouse talks on and on? You've heard it so many times you could repeat it almost word-for-word. Silence and overtalk are typical communication problems that occur occasionally for some, but continually for others. Some people believe their problem is a lack of communication. That is doubtful, for we all communicate in one way or another. Even silence is a form of communication.

A wife was overheard saying to her husband, "I know you believe you understand what you think I said, but I'm not sure you realize that what you think you heard is not what I meant." Mistakes in verbal communication can be as confusing as our mistakes in written communication.

In the classified ad section of a small-town newspaper, the following ad appeared on Monday:

"FOR SALE: R. D. Jones has one sewing machine for sale. Phone 958 after 7 p.m. and ask for Mrs. Kelly who lives with him cheap."

On Tuesday: "NOTICE: We regret having erred in R. D. Jones' ad yesterday. It should have read: One sewing machine for sale. Cheap. Phone 958 and ask for Mrs. Kelly who lives with him after 7 p.m."

On Wednesday: "R. D. Jones has informed us that he has received several annoying telephone calls because of the error we made in his classified ad yesterday. His ad stands corrected as follows: FOR SALE: R. D. Jones has one sewing machine for sale. Cheap. Phone 958 after 7 p.m. and ask for Mrs. Kelly who loves with him."

Finally on Thursday: "NOTICE: I, R. D. Jones have no sewing machine for sale. I smashed it. Don't call 958 as the telephone has been taken out. I have not been carrying on with Mrs. Kelly. Until yesterday she was my housekeeper, but she quit."

As you can see, correct communication is important. You cannot have a relationship with others without good communication. Communication is the process of sharing yourself verbally and nonverbally so that the other person can both accept and understand what you are sharing. But that is only half of good communication. The other half is listening.

THE IMPORTANCE OF COMMUNICATION

The importance of communication is shown in a study that compared happily married couples with unhappily married couples. Results indicated that the happily married couples:

1. talked more to each other;
2. conveyed the feeling that they understood what was being said to them;
3. had a wider range of subjects available to them to talk about (Try this experiment: make an agreement with your spouse not to talk about the children or work for three days. What else would you have to discuss?);
4. preserved the communication channels and kept them open no matter what happened;
5. showed more sensitivity to each other's feelings;
6. and made more use of supplementary nonverbal techniques of communication.[1]

The importance of communication is stressed by many professionals who deal

---

1. C. Broderick, ed., *A Decade of Family Research and Action* "Marital Happiness and Stability: A Review of the Research in the Sixties" (National Council on Family Relations, Minneapolis, Minnesota, 1970) p. 67.

with couples facing marital problems. One writer said, "If there is any indispensable insight with which a young married couple should begin their life together, it is that they should try to keep open, at all cost, the lines of communication between them."[2]

He also wrote, "Communication is essential to the expression of love and indeed to life itself. Where there is love, there must be communication, because love can never be passive and inactive. Love inevitably expresses itself and moves out toward others. When communication breaks down, love is blocked and its energy will turn to resentment and hostility."[3]

HOW WELL DO YOU COMMUNICATE?

To test your own communication skills, write down your response to the following everyday events. Be sure to write your initial response—the first thing that comes to mind—because it probably represents what you would actually say.

2. Reuel Howe, *Herein Is Love* (Valley Forge, Pa.: Judson Press, 1961), p. 100.

3. Howe p. 99.

1. It's Saturday. Your spouse asks you to shop for something but you really don't want to go. You say:

2. You are trying to watch your favorite TV program but your spouse is continually interrupting and asking you questions. The program is at the crucial part and you don't want to miss it. You say:

3. You are describing to your spouse the most exciting event of the day. Right in the middle of it your spouse yawns and says, "I think I'll go get a cup of coffee." You say:

4. Your spouse serves you breakfast. You notice that the bacon is overcooked, which you don't like. The toast is served lightly toasted with fresh butter which is exactly what you like. You say:

5. After dinner your spouse asks you if you would do the dishes tonight since he or she is so tired. You, too, are tired and were looking forward to relaxing. Usually you both do them together. You say:

6. You have just had an argument with one of the children and you realize that you are wrong. It is not easy to apologize to family members because they usually rub it in. You say:

It is possible to communicate in such a manner that others will listen to you and respond. It takes work. You will have to change habit patterns of communication which have been forming for many years, but it can be done.

Most married couples have similar communication complaints. I have a list called "The Dirty Dozen." These are the most common complaints I hear in my counseling. But before you read about The Dirty Dozen, you and your spouse should evaluate your present communication. As you read the following list of behaviors, place a check by each of the items that describe your behavior. Then write an explanation (either in the book or on a separate piece of paper) of how you believe this behavior affects your spouse. Your spouse will also complete this evaluation. Remember, you are not indicating which of these items your spouse does! This is a time for self-evaluation and not other-evaluation.

After both of you have finished, sit down together face-to-face and follow these instructions: The husband should choose one of the items and say to his wife, for example, "I feel that I talk excessively." (These words are very important for this process.) The wife should respond by saying, "I agree that you feel that way." (She is not agreeing that what he said is factually true, but that he feels it is true.) Then she should say, "What do you suggest we do about it?" The husband can respond with why he thinks he does it. Then the wife can offer a positive suggestion or alternate behavior. The process continues with the wife choosing one of the items that applies to her and following the same pattern.

> Excessive talking
> Silence
> Monotone voice
> Big or abstract words
> Long prefaces
> Speaking on a cliche level
> Overly critical attitude
> Speaking for the other person
> Belittling the other person
> Changing the subject
> Yelling
> Nagging
> Nervous laughter
> Smiling when hurting

Avoiding eye contact
Poker face
Suppressing anger
Pretending sleep when the other is
    talking
Over-involvement outside family
TV absorption
Pretending not to hear
Mechanical affection
Faces the other direction when talking
Daydreaming
Denial
Running away from problems
Refusal to think or talk about it
Takes it out on someone or something
Accuses other of self's probelm
Locks it inside
Rationalization or makes excuses
Peace at any price

THE DIRTY DOZEN

I. Gunpowder Words

The first member of the group called *The Dirty Dozen* is the use of what I call inflammatory or gunpowder words. There are many words that fit into this category but they appear to have one thing in common. They cause an explosion of emotions that hurt the other person. Statements like the following are familiar: "Hello pudge, how's the diet?" "Do you have to associate with those delinquents?" "How long are you going to postpone cleaning the garage this year?" "Well, I see you're going to waste your time again this Saturday playing golf." "You're crude." Words such as these can set off angry reactions in the other person. And most of the time the person chose to use the words knowing well the reaction which would occur.

Other words such as "never," "always," and "all" sometimes incite quarrels and disagreements. "Why are you *always* late coming home from work?" "You have *never* listened to me when I've told you about this." "*All* men are like that—they're animals." These statements are exaggerations of the problem. They are stated as absolute truth, but they really are a distortion of the truth. The other person will probably point out exceptions to what you have just said! And then you end up in a power struggle or a deadlock. Neither of you will be able to convince the other. If a person continues to use this pattern of communication, he will be labeled "unfair" and others may avoid him because he appears unreasonable. These statements make you vulnerable to a counteraccusation that you are lying.

Which gunpowder words do you use in your marriage? Write them down. Who uses them? If you know these are explosive words, can you give an adequate reason for continuing to use them? Write a substitute word or phrase that you could use in place of these words.

Words are powerful and have great impact upon ourselves as well as upon others. The saying, "Sticks and stones will break my bones but words will never hurt me," simply is not true! It is a lie! Words *do* affect us. Scripture speaks of the power of our words: "But no one can tame the tongue; it is a restless evil and full of deadly poison. With it we bless our Lord and Father; and with it we curse men, who have been made in the likeness of God; from the same mouth come both blessing and cursing. My brethren, these things ought not to be this way" (James 3:8-10, NASB). "Death and life are in the power of the tongue, And those who love it will eat its fruit" (Prov. 18:21, NASB). " 'How long will you torment me, And crush me with words?' " (Job 19:2, NASB).

II. Silence

A second major communication problem is withheld words, undertalk, superficial talk, or silence. Each of these is a manifestation of the same problem. This type of behavior includes ignoring the other person, pouting, sulking, not responding to questions or comments, the silent treatment, or communicating on the safest or most superficial level possible. There are consequences to this type of nonresponsiveness. Withheld words create doubts. Not saying enough creates confusion. Silence can communicate many possible ideas. It can communicate satisfaction and mutual acceptance or even love, but most of the time it communicates an "I don't care" attitude, contempt, indifference, and coldness.

Don't retreat into silence! The silent treatment is very frustrating.

When a family member is silent, his silence may not be intended as the silent treatment. Perhaps he cannot express himself verbally at this time. In many families one spouse is very talkative, verbal, and expressive while the other is quiet, sedate, and reserved. The verbal one wants to talk: "Come on, talk to me. Let's deal with this particular problem." But the quiet one backs off and becomes less talkative. The verbal one applies more pressure: "I'm going to make you talk!" And the quiet one inwardly says, "Oh, no you're not!" The more pressure that is applied, the deeper the other person is driven into silence.

What can be done when one person refuses to talk? One woman said she told her husband, "I'm willing to listen to you and when you're ready to talk about it, just let me know." That's all she said. She backed off and let him come to the place where he wanted to talk.

But when the other person begins to talk to you, be sure you listen and don't make value judgments. For example, consider the person who approaches his spouse and says, "I'd really like to know what you have to say—come on, talk to me." When the spouse comes to the place where he is willing to open up and talk, the other person says, "That's a dumb thing! Where did you get a stupid idea like that?" Do you think this person will venture out again? Trust has been violated in their relationship.

In his book *Why Am I Afraid to Tell You Who I Am?* John Powell states that we communicate on five different levels, from shallow cliches to deep personal comments. Hang-ups, such as fear, apathy or a poor self-image keep us at the shallow level. If we can be freed from our restrictions, we can move to the deeper, more meaningful level.

The five levels of communication are:

Level Five: Cliche Conversation. This type of talk is very safe. We use words such as "How are you?" "How's the dog?" "Where have you been?" "I like your dress." In this type of conversation there is no personal sharing. Each person remains safely behind his defenses.

Level Four: Reporting the Facts About Others. In this kind of conversation we are content to tell others what someone else has said, but we offer no personal information on these facts. We report the facts like the six o'clock news. We share gossip and little narrations but we do not commit ourselves as to how we feel about it.

Level Three: My Ideas and Judgments. Real communication begins to unfold here. The person is willing to step out of his solitary confinement and risk telling some of his ideas and decisions. He is still cautious. If he senses that what he is saying is not being accepted, he will retreat.

Level Two: My Feelings or Emotions. At this level the person shares how he feels about facts, ideas, and judgments. His feelings underneath these areas are revealed. For a person to really share himself with another individual he must move to the level of sharing his feelings.

Level One: Complete Emotional and Personal Communication. All deep relationships must be based on absolute openness and honesty. This may be difficult to achieve because it involves risk—the risk of being rejected. But it is vital if relationships are to grow. There will be times when this type of communication is not as complete as it could be. [4]

Take the time right now and write down your answer to these questions:

1. What are some of the reasons why a person might respond only at level five or level four?

2. When do you feel most like responding at levels two and one?

3. At what level do you usually respond?

4. At what level does your spouse usually respond?

5. At what level would you like your spouse or children to respond and what could you do to assist them?

---

4. Adapted from *Why Am I Afraid to Tell You Who I Am* by John Powell (Niles, Ill.: Argus Publications), pp. 54-62.

Related to silence and superficial talk is a lack of precise language—vagueness. Precise vocabulary and clearly defined terms are very important, especially when you are expressing expectations and wishes. Not only should you strive to be precise in your own communication, but you should not accept the use of vague words by the person who is talking to you. If someone says, "I'll do it later" or "when I get around to it," that kind of response usually leads to confusion.

The words "I'll try" are vague. Even though they sound good, it is better for a person to say, "I will" if he intends to do something. It is important for you to be specific in your commitments and you should insist that others be specific in their commitments. Instead of saying, "I'll try to get up at 7:00 from now on," say, "I will get up at 7:00." Stating your intention in this form creates a greater level of motivation and you are more likely to follow through with your commitment.

If you happen to live with a person who is a nonresponder, try these suggestions:

When you attempt to engage him in a conversation, call him by his first name and then wait until he has responded before you complete your message. Say his name with an inflection and wait. After he has responded, then share your message. If you know him well, you may want to touch him gently on the arm at the same time.

Avoid the typical complaint usually leveled at a nontalker such as "Why don't you ever talk to me?" or "Can't you say something?" Try some of these questions for openers:

1. "What do you think about . . . ."
2. "Is there something that I'm doing that makes it difficult for you to share this or discuss this with me?" (If the person says yes, be sure you don't become defensive. Listen!)
3. "I notice that you are silent much of the time. Is there something that you are trying to tell me by your silence?"
4. "I'd like to talk with you about your silence and the effect that it has upon me."

Now and then you run into a person who is an "egg-walker." He avoids open and honest discussions for fear of reprimand from others. This person ignores certain subjects or topics and learns to say only what is sufficient to get along. This type of communicator may exist on the level five or cliche level. He gingerly walks around issues or problems. He seeks to avoid conflicts, and yet by "egg-walking" he actually builds up greater potential for more serious conflicts. When feelings are bottled up, they become stronger. Refusing to deal with the issues actually shows a lack of trust of one's partner.

Ecclesiastes 3:7 states that there is a time to speak and a time to be silent. But some spouses choose to be silent all of the time. Their silence creates a barrier for both individual and marital growth.

III. A Discouraging Word

A third major problem in communication is abusive talk or discouraging words. Many Christian homes today are citadels of criticism. Words which tear down a person do not correct a problem but usually intensify it and help to lower the self-esteem of the other person. Typical comments are, "Anyone could have done that. It's not so special." "You may not be pretty but beauty isn't everything." "How can you be so stupid? A two-year-old could have done better than you did." When you engage in attributing insulting characteristics to another person, you are engaging in a process called character assassination.

How does your response affect family members? Are they helped by the statements? Does your message give them insight on what they may have done that was wrong? Will they be able to do a better job next time? Telling a person that he is stupid or dumb for his lack of ability to pound a nail straight doesn't teach him to hammer it correctly. Yelling at one's wife for her being late or telling your friends about it in her presence doesn't help her to be on time.

The Word of God has an answer for this: "Stop being so critical of one another. If you must be critical, be critical of yourself and see that you do not cause your brother to stumble" (Rom. 14:13, Phillips). The scripture also tells us to "encourage one another" (I Thess. 5:14).

". . . criticism must be discriminate and take into account the fact that no human being is perfect and that there are many matters which are so unimportant that they should be ignored . . . . When criticism becomes indiscriminate it is called fault-finding and it leads to most destructive consequences . . . .

"(These) are the factors which make faultfinding so destructive . . . .

"1. Faultfinding is destructive because of its very definition. It is defined here in terms of communications as a way of saying: 'I do not accept you as a human being because I will not recognize in practice and in daily living that human beings are imperfect.' In other words, faultfinding expresses a lack of acceptance of people and a distorted view of reality.

"2. Because of the basic lack of acceptance involved, faultfinding ruins human relationships, makes people feel hostile toward each other, sours the daily atmosphere of the home and makes it a place of misery rather than of happiness and satisfaction.

"3. Faultfinding is destructive not only to the 'victims' (many of whom are not as innocent as it may appear), but to the faultfinder himself or herself, as well. That is because faultfinding makes the other person either turn you off completely, counterattack or store up resentment against you . . .

"4. It follows that faultfinding is an ineffective method for changing the behavior of others. It may produce initial results, but if it is kept up it will lead to the other person not really hearing what you are saying; he may hear it in a mechanical sense but it will soon 'go out through the other ear.' Rest assured, however, that the lack of acceptance involved is received and understood.

"5. Thus, faultfinding can be dangerous because when the time comes that you have a truly necessary and important criticism to make, you are powerless then, having diluted the effectiveness of your arguments in advance so that they no longer mean anything to the person being criticized. The danger is especially apparent in the case of children who—through faultfinding—have been taught to think: 'Never mind, it's just that cranky old parent-faultfinder putting on his broken record again.'

"6. Faultfinding teaches unreasonableness and intolerance. Since it induces distaste, it may lead the other party (spouse, child, employee, etc.) to become unreasonable in the other extreme by becoming especially careless and making an excessive number of mistakes, thus setting up a neurotic interaction . . . .

"7. Faultfinding is a consequence of reliance on certain destructive defense mechanisms. The typical faultfinder either projects his own shortcomings onto another person or displaces his anger toward one person (e.g., boss) onto another (e.g., wife). Most often, faultfinding is an unconscious way of trying to hide one's own weaknesses by projecting them onto someone else . . . ." [5]

If you do have a legitimate complaint or criticism to make, be specific. Listed here are the five most frequent communication gripes of husbands and wives based on a study of 792 couples. [6] The husbands' complaints were: wife nags me, wife is not affectionate,

---

5. Sven Wahlroos, *Family Communication* (New York: Macmillian Publishers, 1974), pp. 20, 21.
6. E.W. Burgess, J.J. Locke, and M.M. Thomas, *The Family* (New York: Van Nostrand Reinhold, 1971).

wife is selfish and inconsiderate, wife complains too much, and wife interferes with hobby. The wives' complaints were: the husband is selfish and inconsiderate, he is untruthful, he complains too much, he does not show his affection, and he does not talk things over.

Let us analyze these complaints by considering one complaint from the wives' report: my husband is selfish and inconsiderate. The complaint, as stated, is very general. If a wife were to say that to her husband, he wouldn't really know what was bothering her. The complaint is not specific because it does not state what behavior was selfish and inconsiderate. The first principle to remember in making a complaint is to make it specific. Also document your complaint with behavioral data. Here are some specifics which amplify this same complaint.

"You never ask me how my day was."

"You rarely give me a compliment."

"You don't offer to help me with the meal or dishes."

"You didn't say a word about the birthday present I gave you."

"You come into the family room and turn the TV channel to the game when I'm in the middle of a program."

"You don't show me much affection unless you want sex later on."

Not only should the complaint be specific, but also it should be in the form of a positive suggestion rather than a direct attack. Consider the positive suggestion given below for the first negative complaint. Then write your own suggestions for each of the remaining statements.

Negative	Positive
"You never ask me how my day was."	"I would appreciate your asking me how my day was."
"You rarely give me a compliment."	
"You don't offer to help me with the meal or dishes."	
"You didn't say a word about the birthday present I gave you."	
"You come into the family room and turn the TV channel to the game when I'm in the middle of a program."	

"You don't show me
much affection unless
you want sex later on."

IV. Sideswipe Words

Another member of *The Dirty Dozen* is
what we call "angle words" or "sideswipe
words." When a vehicle hits another by
scraping along its side, delivering a glancing
blow rather than hitting it head on, we say
the vehicle was sideswiped. Some people
communicate in this fashion. They don't
communicate their thoughts directly. They
try to be subtle. Actually, this is a coward's
approach for they don't want to be held
responsible for the message they are trying
to convey. They don't want the responsibility
or any adverse reaction that might occur.

A parent might say to his teenager, "You
know, most teenagers I know call their
parents if they are going to be late at night."
A husband comments to his wife, "Most
wives I know take some time and fix up for
their husbands when they come home in the
evening," or, "*Her* husband is sure thought-
ful and considerate of her by calling her from
work every day." A message is being
conveyed in these comments but instead of
being direct, the person hints. If confronted,
they will usually deny the double message.

What are the real meanings of the following statements? Wife: "Some wives would be angry at their husband if he came home at 3:00 in the morning." Husband: "Are you mad or something?" Wife: "Oh no, I'm not, but some wives would be."

If you have a complaint to make to your spouse, say it clearly and directly. Be willing to accept the responsibility for what you feel and what you say. If you live with a person who consistently uses this sideswipe approach, don't play his game. Respond at face value to what he is saying and do not respond to the implied message. This may cause him to withhold his comments, or it could cause him to be more specific. The wife could reply to the husband's statement, "Most wives I know take some time and fix up for their husbands when they come home in the evening," by saying, "Why, that's wonderful dear. I'm glad they do and it's nice that you notice that." Say nothing else. But if the very next night you have changed your attire, fixed your hair, and put on some make-up, he soon learns that his subtle messages work. Your response actually reinforces him to continue responding to you in this fashion. It is better to wait for a direct message.

V. Defensive Words

Countercomplaining or defensiveness is

another communication problem. Imagine how you would feel in the following situations.

The husband, exhausted and sitting in a chair, says to his wife, "Am I exhausted—I don't think I've got an ounce of energy left. What a day!" The wife responds, "You think you are tired, let me tell you what it's really like to be exhausted. My day was unreal!" Or, the wife says to her husband as he walks in the front door after work, "Dear, did you stop and pay the bill at the bank today?" Husband: "No I didn't, and before you get upset, remember that you don't get all of your chores and work done either. In fact, take a look at this house."

Countercomplaining and defensiveness which can include attacking the other person verbally) breed irritation, resentfulness, and hurt feelings. Countercomplaining indicates a lack of sensitivity to the needs and hurts of the other person. It cuts deeply at a time when a person is most vulnerable.

When we have been confronted with a failure on our part to fulfill an obligation, we become defensive and resort to recalling the other person's past misdeeds. Bringing up past failures in a discussion about a current problem does nothing to solve the present crisis. Some families have made an agreement with one another whereby they have set a "statute of limitations" on past "crimes." For example, one such rule was that no problem, crime, or fault could be brought up which had occurred more than three months previous. The rule also stipulated that when one person had a complaint directed toward him, he could not respond with a countercomplaint, but must say (whether he agreed with the complaint or not), "Thank you for telling me. What do you suggest that I do?"

Following such a rule may seem contrary to human nature, but with planning beforehand, prayer, and remembering specific scriptural teachings, it is possible. Imagine what a difference there would be in a home atmosphere if the family members would discuss and agree to follow this rule? Often parents ask why their children are so defensive when confronted. The children are more than likely following the example set by their parents.

Here are several scriptures which may help a person to become receptive to the criticism of others. "If you refuse criticism, you will end up in poverty and disgrace; if you accept criticism, you are on the road to fame" (Prov. 13:18, TLB). "Don't refuse to accept criticism; get all the help you can" (Prov. 23:12, TLB). "It is a badge of honor to accept valid criticism" (Prov. 25:12, TLB). "A man who refuses to admit his mistakes can never be successful. But if he confesses and forsakes them, he gets another chance" (Prov. 28:13, TLB).

VI. Emotionalism

Emotionalism includes emotional talk, extensive crying, yelling, and anger. Crying now and then because of hurt feelings and rejection is natural, but using crying to control another person or to end a discussion is emotional talk. Intense, angry tones or even dramatics are used consciously or unconsciously at times. Such behavior could be an honest reflection of how the person is feeling or it could be a ploy to control the conversation.

Disagreements among family members are inevitable. Disagreements can be shared and discussed; it is possible to disagree agreeably. But when anger creeps into a conversation, a disagreement becomes a quarrel. A quarrel has been defined as verbal strife in which angry emotions are in control and participants do not deal with the issues but instead attack the other's personality. A strained relationship marked by continued resentment between the parties usually follows a quarrel.

The Word of God speaks against quarreling. "It is an honor for a man to cease from strife and keep aloof from it, but every fool will be quarreling" (Prov. 20:3, Amplified). "As coals are to hot embers, and wood to fire, so is a quarrelsome man to inflame strife" (Prov. 26:21, Amplified). "Let all bitterness and indignation and wrath (passion, rage, bad temper) and resentment (anger, animosity) and quarreling (brawling, clamor, contention) and slander . . . be banished from you . . ." (Eph. 4:31, Amplified).

VII. Double Level Messages

Have you ever heard of double level messages? They are statements or questions which are intended to mean something other than that which is communicated. When you answer a person with statements like "I guess not," "I'll see," "it doesn't matter," or "later on," what do you mean? What does "later on" mean to you and to the other person? Why do you get upset about something when earlier you said it didn't matter? Some married people have been heard to say later, "Of course it mattered. You should have known what I meant." Parents may remember saying to an adolescent, "I didn't say you could go. I said maybe you could and never really intended to let you go."

Another example is the wife who tells her husband that she doesn't mind his being late for dinner. But her behavior says something else! When he does come home she doesn't speak to him, gives him a plate of cold food, and goes off to watch TV while he eats by himself. The verbal and nonverbal behavior do not match, and the nonverbal component carries much more weight than the verbal component. It is important to state clearly, exactly, and honestly what one means. When we speak in a way that gives another person the wrong impression, confusion is created.

Sometimes people intentionally give the wrong impression because they are afraid of speaking the truth. They are afraid of the confrontation which might occur or they are afraid that someone's feelings might be hurt. Again the scripture speaks about this communication problem. Christians are to grow up "speaking the truth in love" (Eph. 4:15, NASB). Ephesians 4:25 says, "Therefore, rejecting all falsity and done now with it, let everyone express the truth with his neighbor, for we are all parts of one body and members one of another" (Amplified).

Another way in which we can communicate double level messages is by asking questions with an ulterior motive. "How do you like my dress?" or "What did you think of the dinner?" "What did you think of my speech at the business club today?" Is the person asking these questions seeking an opinion or indirectly asking the other to praise him and build him up? If the other person answers honestly, you may be surprised and receive a comment you were not expecting. Is it fair to become upset over an unexpected comment? The other person was probably taking the question at face value and felt you wanted to know his honest opinion. We should not ask a question unless we are willing to hear an honest response. Indirect or devious questions create marital discord.

Good communication requires that couples who are afraid of asking or answering honest questions learn to do so. If someone asks you a double level question, you should answer it at face value. Before giving an answer you might ask, "What are you really asking me? Am I free to give an honest answer to the question or do you have another thought behind it?" If the other person admits there was something else, let him know that you would appreciate honesty in his question because you are not a mind reader and can only respond to the question as stated.

If a family member consistently asks questions in this manner hoping that he will be praised or built up, it could mean that he is not receiving sufficient spontaneous praise from others in the family.

VIII. The Shifty Eye

The eighth problem in our list of the twelve most common communication barriers is the shifty eye, or lack of eye contact. No eye contact (not looking at a person when talking with him) causes confusion and conveys wrong information. In our family communication process, we often fall into the habit of talking to another person from another room, doing two or three things at the same time while carrying on a conversation, or speaking with our back to the other person and/or walking away from him.

Have you ever considered how this affects the communication process? Perhaps the result can best be illustrated by looking at the components of a message.

In our communication, we send messages. Every message has three components: the actual content, the tone of voice, and the nonverbal communication. With changes in the tone of voice or in the nonverbal component, it is possible to express many different messages using the same word, statement, or question. Nonverbal communication includes facial expression, body posture, and actions. An example of nonverbal communication which should be avoided is holding a book in front of one's face while talking.

The three components of communication must be complementary. One researcher has suggested the following breakdown of the importance of the three components.[7] The percentages indicate how much of the message is sent through each one.

Content 7%
Tone 38%
Nonverbal........55%

Confusing messages are often sent because the three components are contradicting each other. When a man says to his wife with the proper tone of voice, "Dear, I love you," but with his head buried in a newspaper, what is she to believe? When a woman asks, "How was your day?" in a flat tone while passing by her husband on the way to the other room, what does he respond to, the verbal or nonverbal message?

A husband, as he leaves for work, comes up to his wife, smiles, gives her a hug and kiss, and states in a loving voice, "I really love you." After he has gone she walks around feeling good. But when she notices a newspaper in the middle of the room,

7. Albert Metowbian, *Silent Messages* (Belmont, Calif: Wadeworth Publishing Co., 1971), pp. 42-44.

pajamas on the bed, dirty socks on the floor, and the toothpaste tube with cap off lying in the sink, her good feelings begin to dissipate. She has told her husband how important it is to her that he assume responsibility for these things, because they make extra work for her. But he has been careless again. She believed him when he left for work, but now she wonders, "If he really meant what he said and really loves me, why doesn't he show it by assuming some responsibility? I wonder if he really does love me." His earlier actions contradicted his message of love, even though it may have been sent properly.

Take a minute and think about how you communicate nonverbally. Describe on paper how you communicate nonverbally in your family. Then write down how your spouse communicates nonverbally. After you have done this, write down what you think your nonverbal communication means to the other person and what you think your spouse's nonverbal communication means. Ask your spouse to do this too and then compare and discuss your responses.

Our nonverbal communication and tone of voice are essential elements in conveying our messages. If you are not aware of your tone of voice, you may want to use a tape recorder to record some of your conversations. Then play it back and pay attention to your tone of voice and what it implies.

Concerning nonverbal communication, Dr. Mark Lee said, "Marital problems may grow out of unsatisfactory nonverbal communications. Vocal variables are important carriers of meaning. We interpret the sound of a voice, both consciously and subconsciously. We usually can tell the emotional meanings of the speaker by voice pitch, rate of speech, loudness, and voice quality. We can tell the sincerity or insincerity, the conviction or lack of conviction, the truth or falsity of most statements we hear. When a voice is raised in volume and pitch, the words will not convey the same meaning as when spoken softly in a lower register. The high, loud voice, with rapid rate and harsh quality, will likely communicate a degree of emotion that will greatly obscure the verbal message. The nonverbal manner in which a message is delivered is registered most readily by the listener. It may or may not be remembered for recall. However, the communicator tends to recall what he said rather than the manner of his speech."[8]

Is your own nonverbal communication warm or cold? Here is a brief list that may help you determine the effect it has on people.

8. Gary Collins, ed., *Make More of Your Marriage* (Waco Texas: Word Books, 1976), From an article by Dr. Mark Lee, "Why Marriages Fail - Communication," p. 75.

Nonverbal Cue	Warmth	Coldness
Tone of voice	soft	hard
Facial expression	smiling, interested	poker-faced, frowning, not interested
Posture	lean toward other, relaxed	lean away from other, tense
Eye contact	look into the other's eyes	avoid eye contact
Touching	touch other softly	avoid touching other
Gestures	open, welcoming	closed, guarding oneself and keeping other away
Spatial distance	close	distant

IX. Speaking For Others

Speaking for another person is a problem that is manifested in a number of ways. One way of speaking for others is outguessing another person. A typical situation involves one spouse trying to speak to the other but being interrupted in the middle of every thought. Wife: "Honey, I was down at the store today . . ." Husband: "Oh, you went to the Broadway?" Wife: "No, I didn't say I was at the Broadway. I was at the hardware store and I ran into Howard . . ." Husband: "Howard Smith who used to live across the street?" Wife: "No! It wasn't Howard Smith. Now will you quit interrupting!"

We speak for another person by attempting to say what we think he is thinking, feeling, or intends to say. This is accomplished by "you statements." The process is also called "mind reading." It implies that the person making the "you statements" is an expert on what the other person thinks and believes. "I know you don't want to go." "You really didn't have a good time." "Oh, you don't want to read that book or see that film." "You're too tired to go." Statements such as these, especially with a corresponding tone of voice and nonverbal actions, can elicit negative reactions. Often a spouse uses this manner of speaking to get his point across without taking direct responsibility for what he wants to say. The Minnesota Couples Communication Program has suggested a much healthier model for expressing oneself. The model includes four "Skills for Expressing Self-Awareness."

1. Speaking for self, rather than for others
2. Documenting with descriptive behavioral data

3. Making feeling statements (speaking about oneself)
4. Making intention statements (speaking about oneself)[9]

1. *Speaking for self.*
Husband: "I'd like to go out tonight."
Wife: "I would too. I'd like to eat out at a nice restaurant. How about you?"
Husband: "I think that's a good idea. I'd like to go to . . . ."
The *underresponsible* person doesn't let others know what he wants or feels (or tries not to, anyway). He says things in indirect ways, often making sweeping generalizations about what "everyone" thinks or feels:
"Some wives would be angry at your staying out all night."
"Other guys expect their wives to look good when they go out together."
This type of person is trying to avoid being candid about his own thoughts, feelings, and intentions. Often, he is put in the position of denying his own thoughts, feelings, and intentions, almost as if he were a non-person.
Wife: "Some wives would be angry at your staying out all night."
Husband: "You mad or something?"

9. *Minnesota Couples Communication Program Handbook* (Minneapolis, Minnesota: Minnesota Couples Communication Program, 1972), pp. 23-31.

Wife: "Oh no, I'm not. But some wives would be."

Another type of person, the *overresponsible* person, also leaves out the "I." But his problem is trying to speak for others. So he tells them what they think or feel or intend. To do this, he usually sends "you messages":

"You don't like that kind of TV program."

"You're pretty tired tonight, aren't you?"

"You want to go on a fishing trip this year, don't you?"

When you speak for someone else, you proclaim that you are an expert on what he thinks, feels, or intends. You tell him that you *know* what is going on in his mind— maybe even better than he does. But can you really?

A close variation of speaking for yourself is what is called the "I message." It is very helpful in resolving conflicts. "I messages" are messages from a person which identify where the speaker is and thus are more oriented to the speaker than to the listener. The speaker may want to modify the behavior of another person, to change a situation, or simply identify his position or feeling. An "I message" is distinguished from a "you message" in that the speaker claims the problem as his own.

An "I message" consists of three parts: the feeling, the situation, and how it affects the sender. It is a statement of fact rather than an evaluation and, therefore, is less likely to lower the other person's self-esteem. It is also less likely to provoke resistance, anger, or resentment, and is, therefore, less likely to hurt the relationship. The "I message" is risky because it may reveal the humanness of the speaker and the listener may use this vulnerability against the speaker. But it helps a person to get in closer touch with his own feelings and needs. It models honesty and openness.

2. *Documenting with descriptive behavioral data.* Documenting is *describing*.

"I *think* you're elated. I see a smile on your face, and your voice sounds lyrical to me."

Documenting is an important skill. First, it increases your own understanding of yourself. It gives you a better idea of *how* you arrived at your own thoughts, feelings, and intentions. And at the same time, it gives the other person a much clearer idea of *what* you are responding to.

3. *Making feeling statements.* When you make a feeling statement, you don't know how the other person will respond. So, feeling statements are risky.

Wife: "I feel sick to my stomach when I see you bow and scrape to your boss."

There are four main ways to describe feelings verbally.

(1) Identify or name it. "I feel angry." "I feel sad." "I feel good about you."

(2) Use similes and metaphors. We do not always have enough labels to describe our emotions so we sometimes invent what we call similes and metaphors to describe feelings.

"I felt squelched." "I felt like a cool breeze going through the air."

(3) Report the type of action your feelings urged you to do. "I felt like hugging you." "I wish I could hit you."

(4) Use figures of speech, such as "The sun is smiling on me today," "I feel like a dark cloud is following me around today."

4. *Making intention statements* is a way of expressing your immediate goals or desires in a situation. These statements provide a different kind of self-information to the other person—an overview of what you are willing to do.

Wife: "I *want* very much to end this argument."

Husband: "I didn't know that. I thought you were too mad to stop."

Or another example:

Wife: "Whether we go to New Orleans or Jamaica isn't so important. What I really want is for you to listen to me and take my feelings into account."

Husband: "That surprises me. What I

thought you wanted most was an expensive vacation."

Intention statements can be surprising because so often people think they know what other's intentions are.

Here is an opportunity for you to practice "I messages" with the four skills. Read each situation and the suggested "You message." Then write an "I message." If you and your spouse are reading this together, use separate pieces of paper for this exercise and then compare the results.

Sending "I Messages" vs. "You Messages"

Situation	"You Message"	"I Message"
Wife picks up husband's empty coffee cup from the rug in the family room for the fourth morning in a row. When he arrives home:	"You left your coffee cup in the family room again for the fourth time in a row. You sure aren't making it any easier for me to keep the house looking nice."	
Husband comes home with a new suit he bought on sale. Both had just agreed to avoid extra expenses this month.	"You have no concept of budgeting! We're going to end up so far in debt that we'll never get out because of your careless spending."	

While preparing to make love, husband suggests using a different position for intercourse than the usual one.	"You must be crazy. Only animals or sex fiends do it that way."
Wife suggests that they attend a prayer group which has been meeting regularly at the church.	"You don't really believe in that group prayer stuff, do you?"
Wife tells husband that she talked with her parents on the phone at the office today and invited them to visit this weekend.	"You always make plans without consulting me—particularly with your family."
Husband spanks the three-year-old for the third time in the evening.	"You are really being cruel to that kid! You're going to make him hate you."
Husband initiates lovemaking non-	(Sarcastically) "You really know

verbally, but wife doesn't respond much.	how to make a guy feel good, don't you?''
Wife makes a mistake in subtraction which causes two checks to bounce.	''Can't you do simple mathematics? I guess you know that costs us $12.''

X. Overtalk

Another one of the major communication problems is called overtalk. Nagging comes under this heading. Incessant talking can create as many problems in a family as silence. In fact, one research study indicated that couples who dissolved their marriages complained more often about too much talking than too little talking. Economy of words can be a blessing at times.

Why do people talk too much? There are many reasons. The person could be insecure and feels more comfortable when expressing himself. Or perhaps he doesn't feel that he is getting through to others and wants to make sure they not only hear him but do as he suggests. Perhaps the person he is talking to doesn't respond and he doesn't know if he has been heard. Overtalk is also a way of dominating or controlling another person, a way of expressing anger and frustration, and a way of getting back at another person.

Nagging is a very common complaint in marriages. Often a husband comes in for counseling and says that his wife nags him. I ask what he means by nag. He replies, "Every week she asks me to clean the garage." Now this really doesn't sound much like nagging. It sounds more like reminding, especially if it is a well-expressed request. We need to note the difference between nagging and reminding.

Nagging has been defined as a continual, persistent, critical faultfinding which creates irritation in another person. One person defined nagging as reminding a person to do something when you know he hasn't forgotten. It has also been expressed as inefficiency on our part to promote the desired behavior in another. Nagging is a negative verbal behavior that has very little communication value.

Husbands and wives experience nagging in terms of being continually reminded to do something. Usually the tone of voice indicates the difference between reminding and nagging. Husbands are nagged about taking out the garbage, cleaning the garage, cutting the grass, cleaning the yard, picking up the socks, etc. Wives are nagged about having dinner on time, overcooking the steak, picking up the soap and shampoo in the shower, taking the clothes to the cleaners, etc.

Does nagging accomplish anything? Some say no, but that isn't true. Nagging does bring results, but they are usually negative results. Nagging encourages a spouse to continue to engage in the very behavior he or she is being nagged about. This behavior leads to quarrels and resentment. It also leads the other person to develop a strange malady—a form of deafness known as tuning out the spouse. Nagging is as common as the flu and, just like a communicable disease, it makes all of the family members miserable.

The scripture warns against overtalking and nagging. "Don't talk so much. You keep putting your foot in your mouth. Be sensible and turn off the flow!" (Prov. 10:19, TLB). "He who despises his neighbor lacks sense, But a man of understanding keeps silent. He who goes about as a talebearer reveals secrets, But he who is trustworthy conceals a matter" (Prov. 11:12-13, NASB). "Love forgets mistakes; nagging about them parts the best of friends" (Prov. 17:9, TLB). "It is better to dwell in a corner of the housetop (on the flat oriental roof, exposed to all kinds of weather) than in a house shared with a nagging, quarrelsome and faultfinding woman" (Prov. 21:9, Amplified).

Here are some steps to take to minimize nagging (if you happen to use this method) and steps to take to respond to one who nags you. First, distinguish between nagging and reminding. A reminder remains friendly and there is no tone of irritation, impatience, or anger. Nagging usually involves destructive means of communication such as the use of exaggeration, sarcasm, humiliation, and playing the numbers game. "You never do what I ask you to do!" "I guess it's too much for the big, important executive to clean up our garage." "A moron could remember to follow instructions." "If I've told you once, I have told you a thousand times."

Although people attempt to use nagging as a means of communicating and motivating, it doesn't work. Instead of recognizing this fact and employing a different means, they intensify their efforts and nag all the more!

Nagging can become a habit. When you fail to get another person's attention before speaking to him, he will probably appear to ignore you. When you yell from one room to another without making sure the other person is listening, can you blame him for lack of response? Sometimes he may hear you and sometimes not. If you allow this pattern to continue, he will soon learn that when you ask him to do something, all he needs to do is tune you out, perhaps even pretend not to hear. With practice he may learn not to hear. The end result is that he learns how to control you by not listening.

Another reason for nagging is that we accept ambiguous answers or responses. If a spouse answers a request by saying, "I will do it later," tell him that you don't know what he means by later, and that to avoid any misunderstandings you would like to know the exact time. If remembering has been a problem for the person, suggest writing a reminder note to help him remember. Always insist upon clear communication and definite responses.

Dr. Sven Wahlroos tells the story of a couple who came to see him for counseling. The wife constantly nagged her husband about things that needed to be fixed around the house. He would just postpone them and would not allow the wife to call in anyone to repair these items because he wanted to save the money. An agreement was worked out with the couple. When the wife noticed that something needed to be fixed, she would bring it to her husband's attention and they would discuss it. The husband then had fifteen days in which to fix it. The couple initialed the calendar date so they would remember when they talked about it. During the fifteen days, the wife was not to mention it again, as the responsibility was the husband's. At the end of fifteen days, if the item was not repaired, the wife could call in a repairman to fix it.

One way that a couple can change some of the nagging behavior which occurs is to define and clarify responsibilities for each person. Perhaps questions could be asked such as, "What are the jobs or tasks which need to be done and when should they be done and by whom?" For many couples, discussing responsibilities has helped to solve problems in areas which have been irritants for many years.

Some couples have created a chart describing the division of labor, with jobs and times when they could be done. The purpose of such a chart is to clarify individual responsibilities. Either spouse should comment upon the other's failure to do his or her job.

If you have a tendency to nag and wish to break this pattern of communication, here is a plan that you can follow.

1. Get other people's attention when you are talking to them.
2. Don't do anything while you are talking that might distract their attention.
3. Define in detail what it is that you expect from them.

4. Discuss the request with them so you will know that they understand it.
5. Attempt to get a specific commitment from them. Vague responses can leave both of you frustrated.

You might find a step-by-step procedure helpful in eliminating your nagging. One has been suggested by Dr. Jerry Schmidt in his book *Help Yourself—A Guide to Self Change.*[10] He calls this procedure moving from mountains to mole hills.

Often people say they want to make a change but they talk about it in general, global terms which also seem insurmountable to them. A person says, "I want to stop nagging," could then look at his life and realize he had nagged for fifteen years and conclude, "Forget it. I've done it this long. I won't be able to stop." He is defeated before the procedure is even begun. But if you take your large goal of stopping nagging and turn it into a number of smaller, specific goals, you will feel more like working on the project and you will also be able to measure progress.

Your mountain might be, "I want to eliminate nagging forms of communication

10. Jerry Schmidt, *Help Yourself - A Guide to Self Change* (Champaign, Ill.: Research Press, 1976), pp.9-15.

from my life." First, define nagging *as you see it*. It might involve the number of times you make a statement, your tone of voice, or your nonverbal behavior. Then make a specific list of changes such as the following:

1. I will allow myself to remind a person to do a task twice a week. Before I remind him, however, I will sit down and write out exactly what I will say.
2. I will substitute verbal reminders for the children with written reminders. For every note I write for them, I will ask them to write themselves one.
3. I will not give another person an instruction unless I am looking at him face to face.

Now take this list and add several changes of your own. Perhaps none of the above apply to you but you know what could be done in your situation.

You might say, "But what if I nag twenty-five times a day now? I can't cut it to two a week." No, but make an agreement with yourself that you will cut the number immediately from twenty-five a day to fifteen a day and each day you will eliminate two more. You need to keep track of these. Now perhaps these suggestions sound too mechanical, but remember that research and experience have shown that they work.

XI. Thoughtless Statements

Not thinking before you speak is a constant irritant. Before you talk with another person, think about what you are going to say. Many people begin to talk before their mind is in gear. As a result, they often say the wrong thing. James 1:19 admonishes us to "Be . . . slow to speak" (NASB). Take your time; think it through; get in mind what you are going to say. Proverbs 14:29 says, "He who is slow to anger has great understanding, but he who is hasty of spirit exposes and exalts his folly" (Amplified). Proverbs 21:23 teaches, "He who guards his mouth and his tongue keeps himself from troubles" (Amplified). And we read in Proverbs 29:20, "Do you see a man who is hasty in his words? There is more hope of a (self-confident) fool than of him" (Amplified).

Have you ever felt that your foot was in your mouth? You wished you hadn't said what you just said. You made a slip of the tongue, and there was nothing you could do to correct it. Or all of a sudden one of the family members irritated you and, without thinking, you snapped out with, "Oh, you'll never be able to do that right, will you?" Or, "You're just like your mother!"

Some time ago I found myself in this same situation, not just before one person but before an entire group. I took my daughter and nephew fishing at a nearby lake. We had caught our limit of trout, and had gone out again for some catfish. The catfish were picking the bait right off the hook. I was becoming irritated with one of them. I would cast to the same area and that fish kept taking the bait off the hook. After twenty minutes of this I cast out to the area, stood up and waited for him to bite. He took it and started to run with it. I slammed the reel closed, tensed up every muscle in my body and hauled back on the pole with all my might. I missed the fish, but I tensed up so much that I got a severe cramp in the back of my thigh and up in my rear end. Without thinking, I grabbed that area of my body and yelled out, "Oh, I've got a terrible cramp in my rear!"

Do you know what happens when you yell from a boat on the water? It's like a giant amplifier. There were boats hundreds of yards away and people were turning around grinning and waving. My nephew and my daughter were in the bottom of the boat laughing their heads off, and I was still standing up in view of everyone on the lake. We fished some more and I thought that I had heard the last of that incident. Finally we went into the dock a couple of hours later. Other boats came in and people looked over at me, grinned, and said, "Hey, there's the guy!" I learned my lesson. Think before you say it!

XII. Not Listening

The last problem of major importance in communication is *not listening*. Paul Tournier said, "How beautiful, how grand and liberating this experience is, when people learn to help each other. It is impossible to overemphasize the immense need humans have to be really listened to. Listen to all the conversations of our world, between nations as well as those between couples. They are, for the most part, dialogues of the deaf."[11]

Dr. S. I. Hayakawa said, "We can, if we are able to listen as well as to speak, become better informed and wiser as we grow older instead of being stuck like some people with the same little bundle of prejudices at 65 that we had at 25."[12]

"By consistently listening to a speaker, you are conveying the idea: 'I'm interested in

11. Paul Tournier, *To Understand Each Other* (Richmond Va.: John Knox Press, 1967), p. 29.

12. Dr. Samuel Hayakawa.

you as a person, and I think that what you feel is important. I respect your thoughts, and even if I don't agree with them, I know that they are valid for you. I feel sure that you have a contribution to make. I'm not trying to change you or evaluate you. I just want to understand you. I think you're worth listening to, and I want you to know that I'm the kind of person that you can talk to.' "[13]

The Living Bible expresses these thoughts about listening: "What a shame—yes, how stupid!—to decide before knowing the facts" (Prov. 18:13). "Any story sounds true until someone tells the other side and sets the record straight" (Prov. 18:17). "The wise man learns by listening; the simpleton can learn only by seeing scorners punished" (Prov. 21:11).

"Let every man be quick to hear, (a ready listener,) . . ." (James 1:19, Amplified). What do we mean by listening? When we are listening to another person we are not thinking about what we are going to say when he stops talking. We are not busy formulating our response. We are concentrating on what is being said. Listening is also complete acceptance without judgment of what is said or how it is said. Often we fail

---

13. George E. and Nikki Koehler, *My Family: How Shall I Live With It* (Chicago, Ill.: Rand McNally and Company, 1968), p. 57.

to hear the message because we don't like the message or the tone of voice. We react and miss the meaning of what was being shared.

By acceptance, we do not mean that you have to agree with everything that is being said. Acceptance means that you understand that what the other person is saying is something he feels. Real listening means that we should be able to repeat what the other person has said and what we thought he was feeling when he was speaking to us.

Interrupting another person is one way of showing that we are not really listening. Interruptions can be verbal but the non-verbal interruptions are even more annoying. The impatient look, the sigh, the wandering eyes, the crossing of the arms, the drumming of one's fingers against the chair or table—all of these are basically saying, "Are you through? I'm not really listening and I want to talk."

Our not listening can help the other person actually become a compulsive talker. Joyce Landorf explains: "Your wife may be a compulsive talker. Was she always that way, even before you were married? Or did she just seem to get that way with time? Some women talk at the moment of birth and a steady stream follows each moment of their lives forever after, but others have developed a nonstop flow of talk for other reasons. Many times a compulsive talker is really shouting to be heard by someone. The more bored you look, the more you yawn, the more you watch the dog or TV, the harder she talks. She just talks all the more to compensate. You may have stopped listening a long time ago, and she knows that better than anybody.

"Do you think this has happened to you? When was the last time that you asked these questions of your wife? 'How do you feel about . . .?' and/or 'What happened here at home today?' Do you ever intersperse her remarks with, 'You may be right, Hon.' If your wife feels you are not willing to listen to her, she has two options: to talk louder and harder; or to talk less and withdraw. Either way, it's very hard on the marriage." [14]

Sometimes you may have to take it upon yourself to get the other person's attention in order to have him listen to you. When our daughter was about six, she came home from school after an exciting day. I was reading the paper and she came up next to me and started to tell me what was so exciting. But I kept on reading the paper. About every ten seconds I'd say, "mmm hmm, fine, yep,"

14. Joyce Landorf, *Tough and Tender* (Old Tappan, New Jersey: Fleming H. Revell Co., 1975), pp. 76,77.

while she was telling her story, but I wasn't listening. All of a sudden there was dead silence—not a word. She stopped talking. A few seconds later a little hand came right down in the middle of my newspaper and pressed it down. I looked up and about a foot from my face there she was looking at me eyeball to eyeball. When she had my attention, she began again at the beginning of her story and told me once again every detail. She knew she had to have my attention first.

Sometimes we think we are giving other people our undivided attention, but we are not giving them sufficient time. I travel during the year, and I may, during the course of a year, take fifteen or twenty trips to different parts of the country for seminars. I usually arrive home on a Saturday night quite tired. But the family hasn't seen me for a couple of days and they like to talk.

I returned home one night and discovered that Joyce had taken our daughter out to get a new coat. We had promised her one and while I was gone, she bought it. As soon as my car pulled into the driveway, my daughter was out the door with her new coat on. She said, "Daddy, look at my new coat! Isn't it neat? Isn't it great?" I looked at it for a few seconds and said, "Yes, that really looks fine, Sheryl."

We got inside the house, finally, and she whirled around in her new coat again and said, "Daddy, do you like the coat? How does it look?" "It looks fine, Sheryl," and I walked off to the other room. About an hour later we were all sitting together in the family room talking and Sheryl turned and said in a quiet voice, "Daddy, even though you didn't look at my coat a long time, do you really like it?" We might think the amount of time that we spend is sufficient for the other person, but maybe it isn't.

There they are—*The Dirty Dozen*—twelve of the major communication problems.

How important is communication? It has been said that communication is to love what blood is to the body; it gives life! But we must make it happen. You must practice new techniques and methods to break old habits. If you begin to change and continue to improve your own methods even if your spouse or children do not respond in the way you hoped they would, the old habits will disappear.

DISCUSSION IDEAS AND QUESTIONS

If you and your spouse are interested in improving your communication together, practice and discuss the methods you have read. Read them again. Then discuss together the series of questions which have been provided, taking turns to answer each question.

1. If my spouse could change one thing about me, it would be_____.
2. What is one thing that you wish your spouse would do more often?
3. If you could ask Jesus to change one thing about your family life, what would it be?
4. My marriage is best when I_____.
5. In my marriage, I am most upset by____.
6. Can you tell if your spouse is upset? How?
7. How would you like to see your marraige improved?
8. Describe a constructive argument.
9. What is the best way that you settle the differences in your marriage?
10. My mate and I have some differences over _____.
11. Is it easy for you and your spouse to pray together? Why?

12. How has your marriage developed in a positive way since you were first married?
13. Something that really upsets me is_____.
14. Who do you feel is the more dominant in your marriage? How is this exhibited?
15. Describe one goal that you have for your marriage.
16. Do you ever interrupt family members when they are talking? Describe what happens.
17. Three reasons why I married my spouse are_____.
18. Describe your marriage as you experienced it during the first year.
19. What do you and your spouse enjoy doing the most together?
20. Describe the funniest thing that ever happened to you in your marriage.
21. How would your mate describe your marriage to your friends?
22. Face your spouse and complete this statement: "What I appreciate about you is _____."
23. If we are married and our mate does something that bothers us, we should tell him or her and try to change it?
    Agree?_____Disagree?_____
24. What are three hindrances to good communication in your marriage?
25. Is it hard to understand your spouse's feelings and attitudes? Why or why not?

26. In what way does your spouse try to lift your spirits when you are depressed or discouraged?

27. When was the first time you were aware that God loved you?

28. When was the first time that you were aware that your spouse loved you?

29. Marriage is a 50-50 proposition.
      Agree?_____ Disagree?_____

30. As I pray for my mate this week, I will pray for_____.

31. How do you think your spouse would describe your marriage?

32. What does your mate do to make you feel loved?

33. What expectations does God have for your marriage?

34. Describe a recent disagreement. What did you do to resolve it?

35. Describe the best spiritual experience that you and your spouse have had together.

36. Who exerts most of the influence over finances in your home and why?

37. How does your spouse show you that he or she is really listening to you when you are speaking?

38. Would your spouse say that you are a better "talker" or a better "listener?" What makes you think so?

39. In what ways has marriage given you freedom?

40. What is the greatest strength you brought to your marriage?

41. What is the greatest weakness you brought to your marriage?

42. I feel most like communicating with my spouse when_____.

43. List three things about your partner's parents that you really like.

44. As far as our marriage is concerned, our in-laws need to learn right now_____.

45. Discuss what kind of family vacation you would like to go on this year.

46. It is wrong for a wife and a mother to have a career. Agree?____ Disagree?____

47. Do you think everybody should marry? Why?

48. Describe what you like to daydream about.

49. What do you want said about you when you have died?

50. What qualities in Jesus would you like to have in your life?

51. When was the last time you cried and what was it about?

52. I wish my children would_____.

53. I wish our family were not_____.

54. I wish more than anything that_____.